HOW

Does a computer remember things?

Om KIDZ
An imprint of Om Books International

AF516733

Contents

How does a computer work?

By following the input, store, process and output cycle! The computer does its primary work in the control centre also called the CPU. When we give any instruction to the computer, it carries out our instructions and converts the input to output.

Find out

What was the Analytical Engine?

1 MHz means 1 million cycles per second

Pocket fact

Faster and Faster!

Every year computers get faster and faster, but do you know someone predicted this already? He is Gordon Moore and his law is called Moore's Law. It says that every two years the speed of the central processor will double.

How many calculations can a computer perform per second?

It varies from one computer to another! The speed of a computer depends upon its processor. The speed at which the processor executes each instruction or each vibration of the clock is called clock speed. The processor requires a fixed number of clock ticks, or cycles, to execute each instruction. The clock speed is measured in MHz. 1 MHz means 1 million cycles per second, 1 GHz means 1 thousand million cycles per second and so on.

How many kinds of memory does a computer have?

A computer has two types of memory: RAM (Random Access Memory) and ROM (Read-only Memory.) RAM is the short term memory that a computer uses for immediate tasks. It stores data and information only as long as the computer is ON. On the other hand ROM, the long term memory holds instructions and data even when the computer is OFF.

Find out

What is a hard disk?

Pocket fact

No ROM!
The earliest computers did not have ROM. When a computer was turned on, it would just do nothing until you entered the commands to start up, using a row of switches on the front of the computer. And if something went wrong, you had to start all over again!

How does a computer memory work?

Memory is the area where a computer stores data. Memory provides the CPU with its instructions. When you switch on the computer or run an application, your operating system allocates space in the RAM and makes the applications run smoothly. ROM stores important control programs and system software to perform a variety of functions, such as starting up programs.

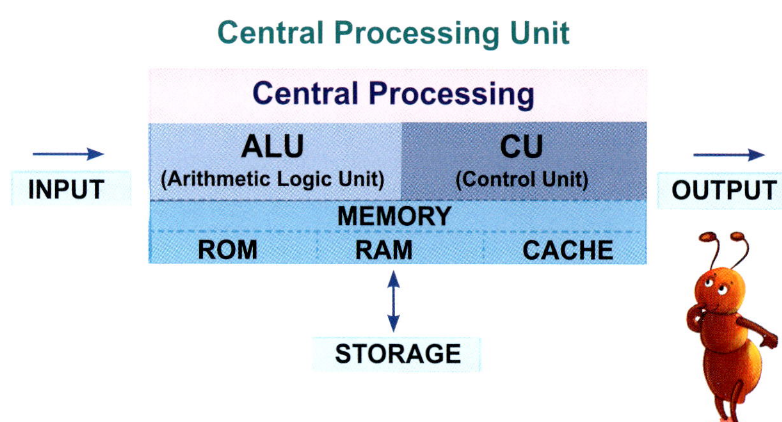

How much memory does my computer really need?

At least 32 megabytes of memory! The amount of memory that you have in your computer is very important. When we talk about memory we mean RAM (Random Access Memory). Most computers have 32 megabytes of memory installed; whereas some have 64 megabytes of memory. If a computer doesn't have enough memory, it may run very slowly or not run some programs at all.

Pocket fact

Random Access Memory!
Computer memory is organized as a bunch of addresses, one per byte. The computer reads or writes to any address in memory without following a sequence. Hence such memory is called Random Access Memory or RAM.

Find out

Why is Read Only Memory or ROM important?

How can I add more memory to my computer?

By putting more RAM in your computer! Sometimes, your computer's hard drive makes a lot of noise and the little hard drive light on the front of your computer flashes a lot while you are using programs. This shows that you need to increase the computer's RAM. To do so, you can ask a computer store to have new RAM chips installed in your computer. This will add more memory to your computer and help it function smoothly.

How is data stored on a computer?

In files and folders! A computer stores a lot of data in files that are actually made up of ones and zeroes, a code that the computer understands! These numbers are called 'bits'. The different ways in which these numbers, or bits, are put together create our files. Eight bits make a byte. Thousand bytes make a kilobyte. Thousand kilobytes make a megabyte and so on. Computer files are stored on a hard drive and you can use them anytime you want.

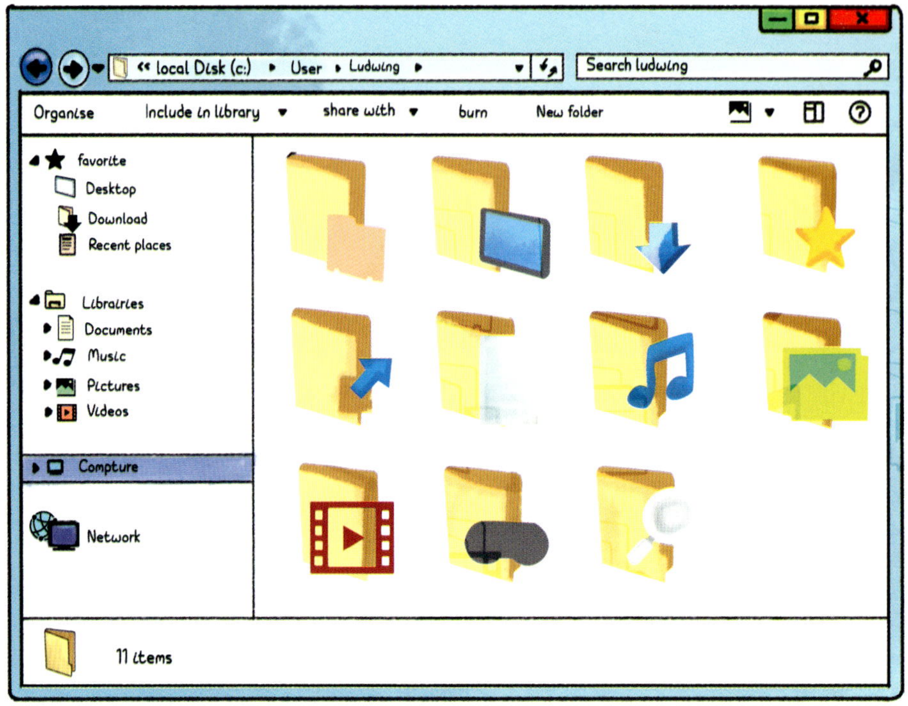

Pocket fact

Only add and subtract!

Not only can your computer count 0 and 1, it is only able to add or subtract. Even though we can do many complex calculations on a computer, deep down inside, the computer is actually only adding and subtracting 0s and 1s.

Find out

How many bytes are there in a gigabyte?

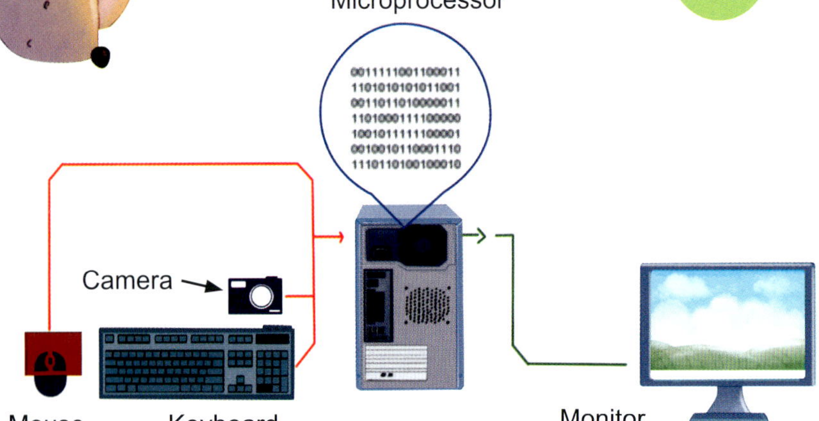

How many bits does a computer use at once?

It depends on what we ask the computer to do! A computer works in 8-bit chunks called bytes. It also works with 16 bits at a time (called a word) or 32 bits at a time (called a long word). When we work with letters, our computer moves bytes at a time. One byte stores one character like a letter, punctuation mark or space.

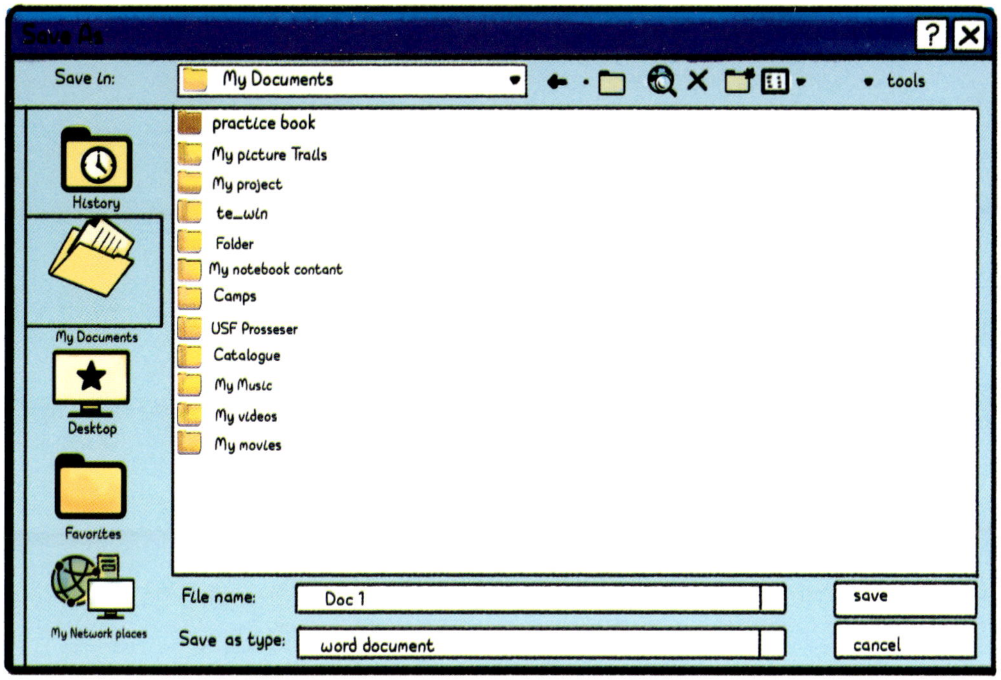

How can I save my work on a computer?

You can do lots of things on a computer. You can make a picture, write a letter or draw a chart. But it is important to save your work if you want to use it later. To save your work you need to give it a name. To do this, click the 'save' button under the file menu and store it safely on your computer.

Pocket fact

No extension!

A file in a computer has an extension. For example: a word document is saved with an extension ".doc". But a folder does not have an extension like a file.

Try it!

Create a folder on your computer desktop and give it any name you like.

How do I create folders on a computer?

We create folders for different documents, files and/or subjects to keep things organized on our computer. To do so, right click in any empty space on your computer. Then, select **New** from the list and it will expand. Select **Folder** from the new list. A new folder is created at the bottom of the list of files and folders with the name **New Folder**. It will be highlighted if you haven't moved the mouse. Type in a name for the folder, e.g. **Lessons**. Press Enter key and the folder will have the new name you typed.

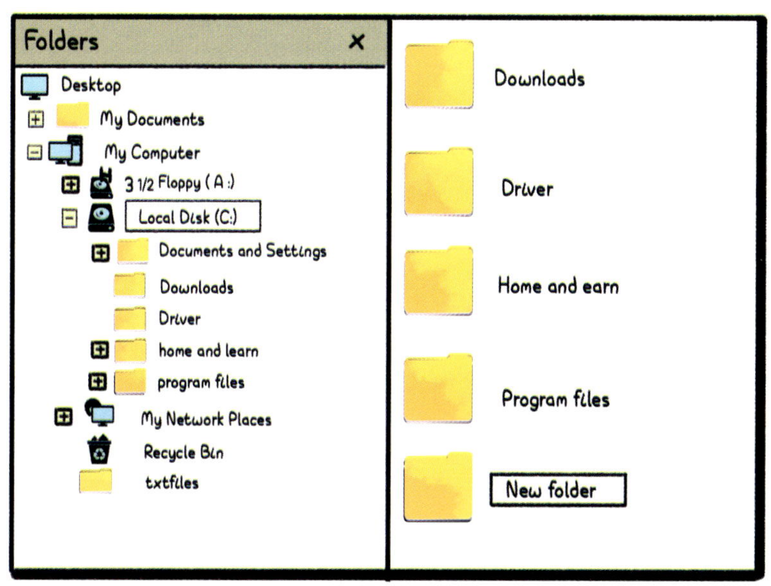

How many languages does a computer know?

Just one! Computers understand only one language which is called machine language or binary language. It is made of only two numbers—0 and 1. We give instructions to a computer in different programming languages. These are translated by the computer into binary codes before the CPU can execute them.

> **Pocket fact**
>
> **High and low-level language!**
>
> Computer languages are of two kinds: high-level and low-level languages. High-level languages are easier to read, write and maintain than low-level languages.

> **Find out**
>
> Do you know any programming languages? Name any two of them.

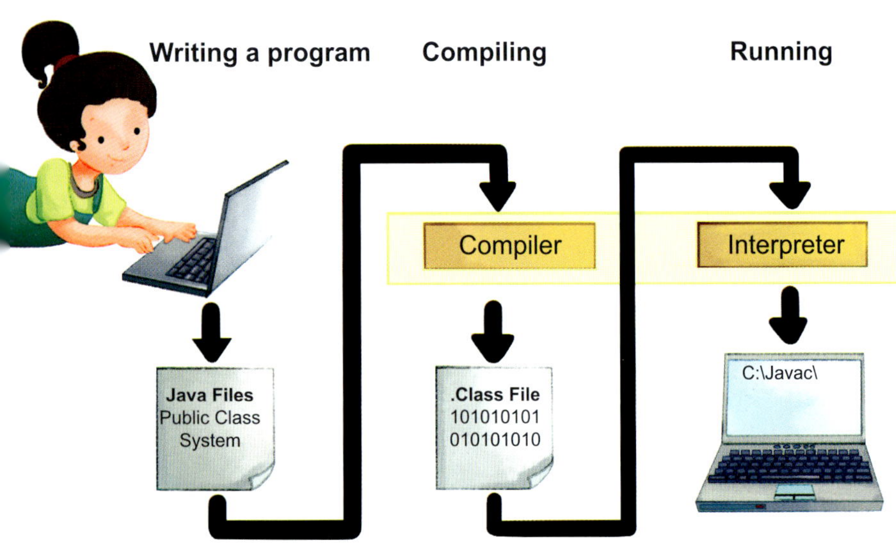

How are our instructions converted into computer language?

With the help of translators called compilers and interpreters! A computer has a piece of translator software which converts our instructions into machine code. These translators are known as compilers and interpreters. Programs are translated using either a compiler or interpreter.

How do computer keys work?

Every keyboard has a key matrix inside it. This matrix is a grid of circuits underneath the keys. When we push a key, the metal part of the circuit connects 2 wires which allow a current to flow to the computer. The computer measures the voltage and transforms the amount of volts into binary codes (0 and 1). The computer compiler reads the binary, and a letter appears on a screen.

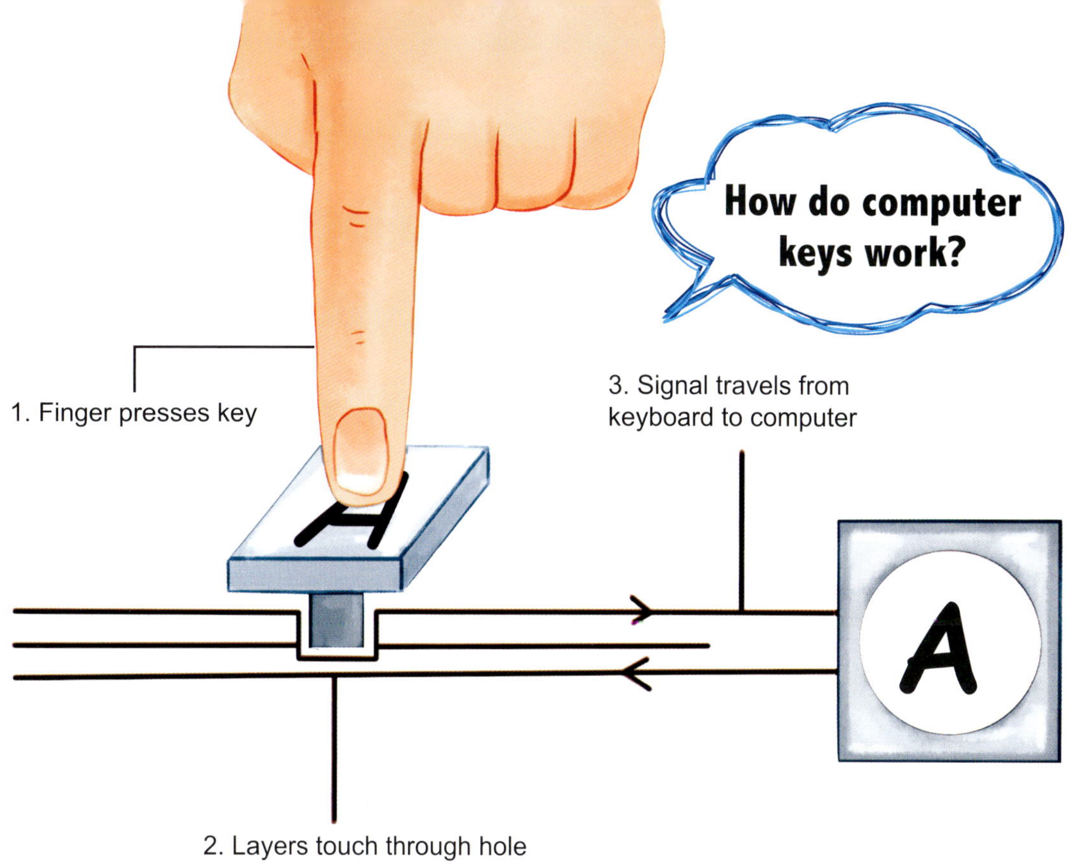

Find out

When do we use the Num lock key?

Pocket fact

Toggle key!
A toggle key is a key that is used to turn a function on or off, or to switch between two functions. Examples of toggle keys are the caps lock key, number lock key and scroll lock key.

How does a wireless keyboard work?

With the help of a battery! A wired keyboard is connected to a computer using a serial port, either by a five-pin serial connection or a USB cable. The keyboard receives power over this cable and transmits the commands to the computer. Whereas, a wireless keyboard is powered by battery and sends its signal to a receiver that is connected to the computer through a USB port.

How does a monitor work?

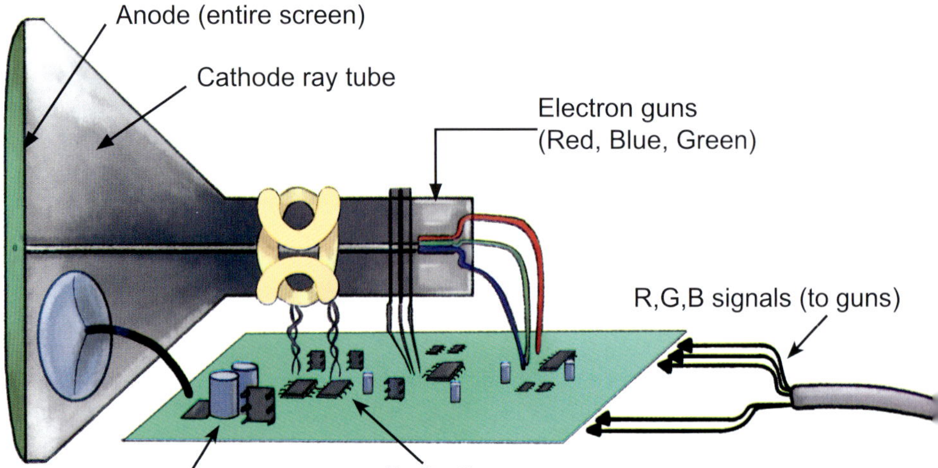

A cable connects the monitor to a video adaptor on the motherboard of the computer. When we work on a computer, the CPU sends instructions to the video adaptor telling what needs to be displayed on the screen. The video adaptor then converts the instructions into signals and sends it to the monitor. The monitor then generates the picture on the screen from the set of signals.

Pocket fact

The First Monitors!
The first computer monitors were modified typewriters and Teletype machines. These devices were slow, noisy and expensive, and could only handle text.

Find out
What is an MP3 file?

How can I hear sounds on my computer?

With the help of speakers and a sound card! A computer usually has speakers and a sound card (a hardware that sends sounds to the speakers) to produce sound. The sound card connects to the motherboard inside the computer. The speakers connect to the sound card through a cable at the back of the computer and help us listen to sounds.

How do different kinds of computer mouse operate?

There are wired computer mouse. There's also wireless computer mouse that use radio signals to transmit to the computer where the cursor is. There's also footmouse that allows users the ability to move the cursor and click buttons with their feet.

Pocket fact

Track Point!
In some laptop computers, almost between the G and H keys, is a small rubber stick called a track point! When you move it around with your index finger, it moves the cursor.

Find out

What is joystick?

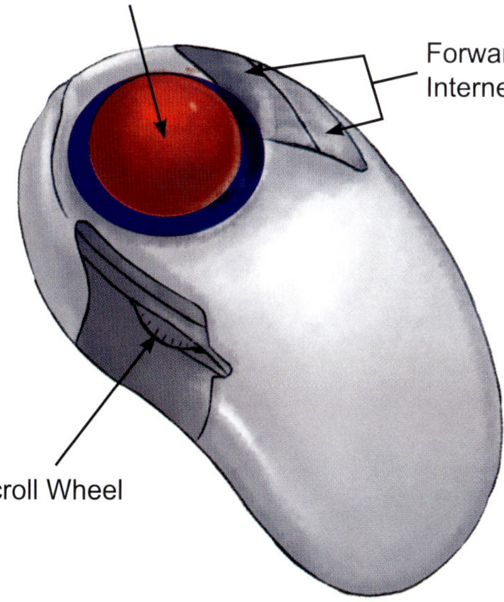

How is a trackball different from a mouse?

A trackball is a stationary pointing device with a ball on its top or side. To move the pointer using a trackball, we rotate the ball with our thumb, fingers or the palm of our hand. Whereas using a mouse, we can move the pointer on the screen to an object such as a button, a menu, an icon, a link or text. Then, we can press a mouse button to perform a certain action associated with that object.

How do computers 'talk' to each other?

By setting up network connections! Computers communicate to each other by means of network. Network connections are set up by wired or wireless means and allow computers to 'talk' to each other and share computing power. There are different kinds of network such as Personal Area Network, Local Area Network, Campus Area Network, Metropolitan Area Network, Wide Area Network, Global Area Network and Internet.

Find out

What is the difference between a web page and a website?

Pocket fact

ARPANET!

In around 1960s when there was no Internet, the Department of Defense, United States created a computer network called the DARPANET. It connected the computers of the department together by a telephone wire. This led to the invention of Internet.

How do computers handshake?

By establishing rules to connect to each other! When a computer communicates with another device like a modem, printer or network server, it needs to handshake with it to establish a connection. To do so, one computer sends a message to another computer indicating that it wants to establish a communications channel. The two computers then send several messages back and forth that enable them to verify the connection, speed or the authorization of the computer trying to connect to it.

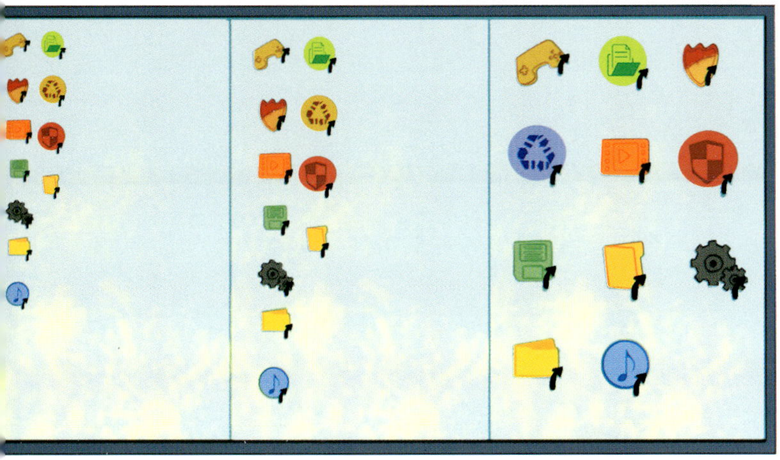

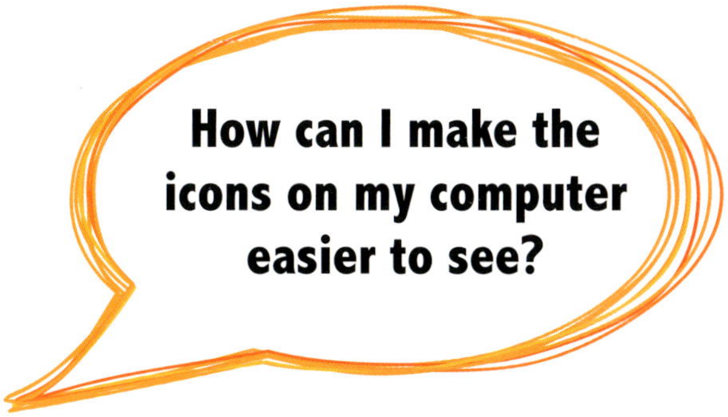

By increasing the size of text and icons! We sometimes find the text on the screen difficult to read. To increase the size of letters and icons, go to the **Control Panel**. Under **Explore all settings**, click to select 'Make the computer easier to see'. Under **Make things on the screen larger**, press **'Alt' + 'Z'** or click to select **'Change the size of text and icons'**. You can change the text and icon size to 100% or 125% depending on your choice. Then click '**Apply**' and press '**Enter**' to accept your changes.

Pocket fact

That's an icon!
An icon (in computing) is a picture which represents a computer program, file, folder, or an action for a program to do. Icons are usually small pictures, but not always.

Try it!

Draw the icon of Recycle Bin found on your computer desktop.

How can I rotate my computer screen?

By using the Ctrl and Alt keys! Some changes in settings can cause your computer screen to turn on its side or upside down. To do so, press and hold the Ctrl and Alt keys while you press the arrow keys. Pressing these keys at the same time will rotate the screen back to the default setting.

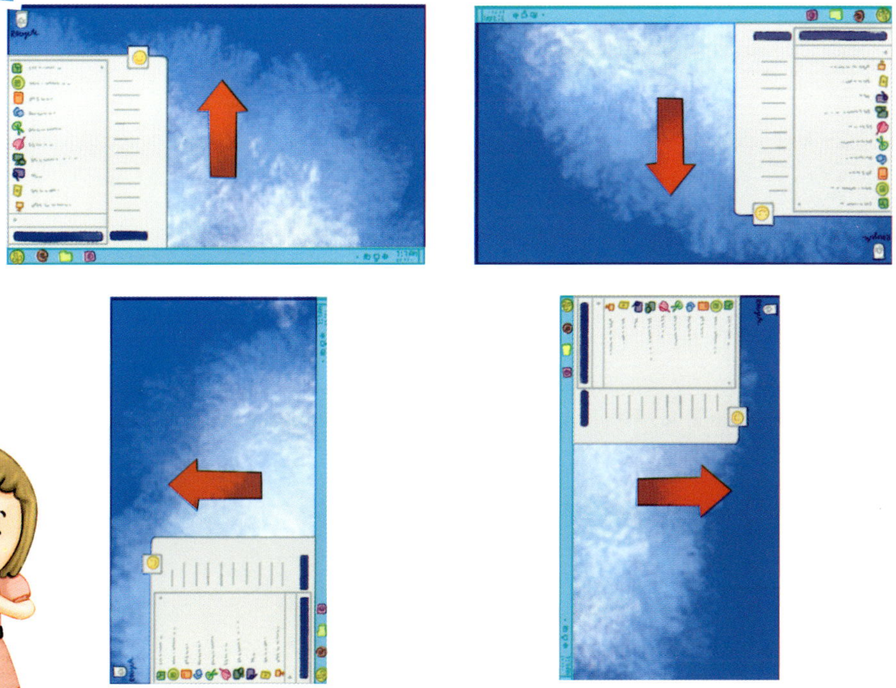

How does a virus harm my computer?

A computer virus is a program created by someone to harm other computers. Viruses are programs that tell your computer to do something destructive. For example, if you start your word processing program, the virus might keep you from starting your computer, or it may delete all of your documents!

Find out

Which antivirus program is installed in your computer/laptop?

Pocket fact

Do not click!

We cannot get a computer virus by just reading an email. A virus is only activated when we click a link or open an infected attachment.

How does an antivirus work?

By stopping computer viruses from harming our computer! An antivirus is a program that can find viruses and stop them from doing bad things to our computer. It protects our computer by monitoring all file changes and the memory for specific virus activity patterns. When these known or suspicious patterns are detected, the antivirus warns the user about the action before they are performed.

How can you use the internet?

Computers have programs called browsers, which are used to access the World Wide Web (www). The web is one of the most important uses of the Internet. There are lots of websites on the Internet. They are made up of web pages. A web page can have videos, pictures, words and games on it.

Pocket fact

HTTP!

When you open a web page, you notice http in the address bar. HTTP refers to Hypertext Transfer Protocol. It is the set of rules for transferring files (text, graphic images, sound, video, and other multimedia files) on the World Wide Web.

Find out

Who invented the email?

How does someone shout in an email?

By writing in all capital letters! When we send an email to someone, he/she can read it but cannot actually hear your message. But an email that is typed in all capital letters, like "HI HOW ARE YOU?" is considered to be shouting! It is considered to be rude so we shouldn't write an email in all capital letters.

Index